The Notebook

A reference manual to help you identify and document the wild horses living wild and free in Theodore Roosevelt National Park

Chasing Horses

2021

Chasing Horses

www.chasinghorses.com

The Notebook: A reference manual to help you document the wild horse herd living wild and free in Theodore Roosevelt National Park. ISBN#9781732272064
Published 2021 by Chasing Horses 312 Pacific Ave., Medora, ND 58645
Website: www.chasinghorses.com email: imchasinghorses@gmail.com
Text and images copyright Christine & Gary Kman

The Notebook is self-published by Chasing Horses
First edition Book design by Christine Kman Text and photographs by Christine & Gary Kman

"A great horse will change your life. The truly special ones define it..."
~Author Unknown

Hello and welcome to the 2021 Notebook!

2020 was a monumental year full of changes for all of us and the horses of Theodore Roosevelt National Park were not excluded!

We have poured our hearts and souls into this book and we truly hope you enjoy it!
What's inside?!

Inside the 2021 Notebook, you will find photographs of every horse currently living in Theodore Roosevelt National Park as of January 2021. The horses are divided into their current bands as of January 2021. Please note that we fully expect there to be MANY changes over the course of the year! Don't worry! We left you plenty of space to take notes!

Each band section gives an overview for that band and highlights from 2020. At your request, we added more and more photos!

We hope that the number of photos that we shared for each band will help you see how much they change especially through the seasons.

There is also a section in The Notebook for the bachelor stallions that gives a summary of their happenings for 2020.

Lastly, there is a memorial section that pays tribute to the horses we lost in 2020.

We hope you enjoy the 2021 Notebook! Be sure to follow us on Facebook and Instagram for the latest updates and information about this herd of horses!

Thank you for your support!

Chris & Gary
Chasing Horses
www.chasinghorses.com

Chasing Horses
www.chasinghorses.com

Table of Contents

Band Stallions

2010 Stallion Arrowhead

2010 Stallion Arrowhead's band consists of:
2004 Mare Little Brother's Girl
2006 Mare Diamond
2006 Mare Domino
2007 Mare Blue
2010 Mare Papoose
2013 Mare Justice
2014 Mare Velvet
2014 Mare Opal
2019 Filly Antice
2020 Filly Frosted Arrow
2020 Filly Betsy
2020 Colt Blackjack

Stallion Arrowhead had a busy 2019 and it showed when he welcomed 2 new fillies and one new colt into his band this year!

Mare Domino gave birth to Colt Blackjack. Mare Papoose gave birth to Filly Betsy. Mare Justice started the 2020 year off with the very first baby of the year: Filly Frosted Arrow.

The last mare that Arrowhead added to his band was Mare Opal in 2018. While he did not add any new mares this year, he was involved in a weird circle with Mare Strawberry and her 2020 Colt Boomer before she passed away this year.

Mare Strawberry spent her last month or so going back and forth between Stallion Arrowhead's band and Stallion Xander's band. To our knowledge, Arrowhead never fought Xander for Strawberry. It may very well be that she and Boomer were left behind from the rest of the band and Arrowhead just kept them safe until they could reunite with the rest of the band.

The once quiet band stallion who kept to himself has rightfully earned the respect of his fellow band stallions. He has also worked hard to keep his band together and is quick to challenge younger stallions who get too close to his band. 2021 should bring some new additions to this band.

2004
Mare
Little Brother's Girl

2006
Mare Diamond

2010 Mare Papoose gave birth to a filly on April 23, 2020.

Papoose & Arrowhead's filly was given the name Betsy.

2006 Mare Domino gave birth to a colt on April 30, 2020.

Domino's colt was given the name Blackjack.

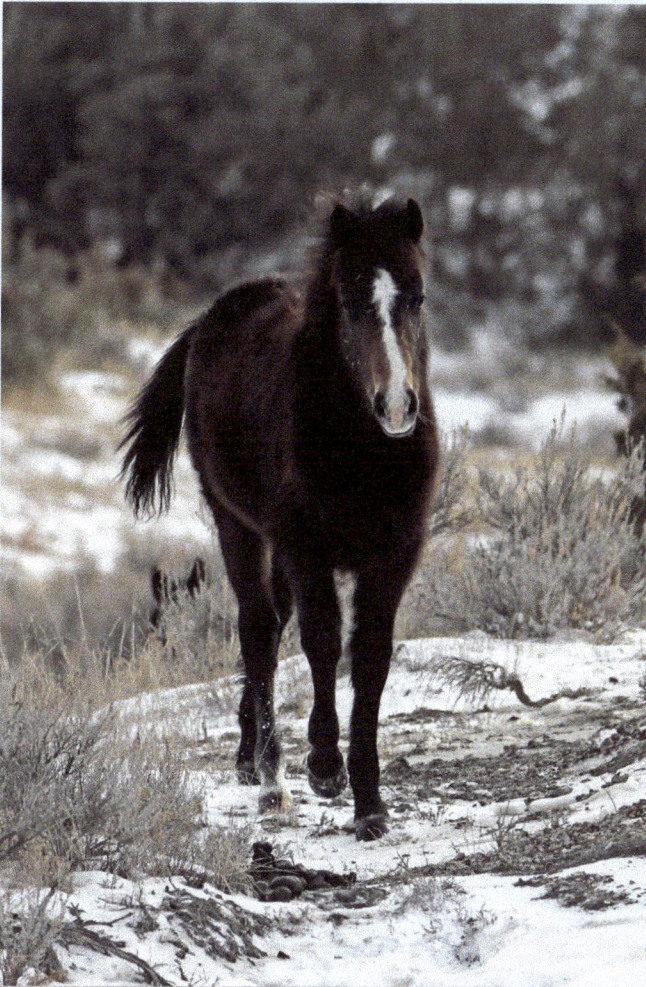

2019 Filly Antice

Mare Domino and Stallion Arrowhead had a filly in 2019. She is the only yearling that was left in this band after the captures in 2019.

Filly Antice is a beauty! She has changed A LOT this year from January (top photo) to December (bottom photo).

2013 Mare Justice gave birth to her first baby AND the very first foal born in 2020 to the TRNP herd on January 11, 2020!! Her frosted little filly was named Frosted Arrow. Stallion Arrowhead is the presumed sire.

Many worried about this little filly's ability to survive the extreme cold weather we were experiencing in January of 2020.

As you can see by the photos on the opposite page, she has not only survived and thrived her first North Dakota winter, but is growing into a beautiful filly!

2013 Mare Justice & 2020 Filly Frosted Arrow

2007 Mare Blue

2014 Mare Velvet

2014 Mare Opal

Chasing Horses
Notes

2004 Stallion Brutus

2004 Stallion Brutus' Band consists of:
2010 Mare Cassie
2013 Mare Dawn
2014 Mare Penny
2014 Mare Paisley
2014 Mare Skipper
2019 Colt Arey

What a start to 2021 for Stallion Brutus!

Brutus had been running as a bachelor since the fall of 2019 when he lost his band to Stallion Maverick.

As we rang in 2021, so did Brutus! In an unexpected turn of events, he managed to take back the majority of his band from Stallion Maverick!

Since this is breaking news as we go to print, there will not be a lot of photos of Brutus with his band. There is still some band news to share:
Mare Penny lost her baby in April.
Mare Maddie broke from Maverick's band in the fall of 2020. She is currently with Stallion Trooper. She was Brutus' lead mare for YEARS! We will see if she reunites with her old love and bandmates!

Time will tell if he is able to hold onto these mares. Stay tuned to our Facebook page for updates on Brutus, Maverick and all of the horses of TRNP!

2010
Mare
Cassie

2013
Mare
Dawn

2014
Mare
Penny

2014
Mare
Paisley

2014
Mare
Skipper

2019
Colt
Arey

Chasing Horses
NOTES

2005 Stallion Coal's Band

2005 Stallion Coal's band consists of:
2000 Mare Busy Blue
2006 Mare Betty Blue
2007 Mare Maggie
2014 Mare Dixie
2019 Colt Amantes

Our first sighting of Stallion Coal in 2020 was when he and Stallion Frontier crossed paths. This was very odd because both bands were in an area quite a distance from where they are usually found.

After that, Coal and his band retreated across the river, as they have since 2018, when Coal and Dixie's 2017 Filly Moana was captured and removed from the park.

Coal usually keeps to himself. His band is usually pretty laid back. Betty Blue presumably lost her baby this year. Her yearling colt, Amantes, became almost inseparable to Mare Maggie. This is a common behavior we have witnessed with mares who had both a yearling and a new foal in 2020. The yearling spent more time with another member of the band, while the new baby got moms attention.

2000
Mare
Busy Blue

2014
Mare
Dixie

2006 Mare Betty Blue and Stallion Coal had a colt in 2019 named Amantes. He is growing to be as handsome as his dad!

Betty Blue is believed to have lost her baby in 2020.

2007 Mare Maggie has developed quite a bond with 2019 Colt Amantes. This has been a re-occurring theme this year as we were able to witness the behavior of the yearlings within the band structure since all captures were postponed due to Covid.

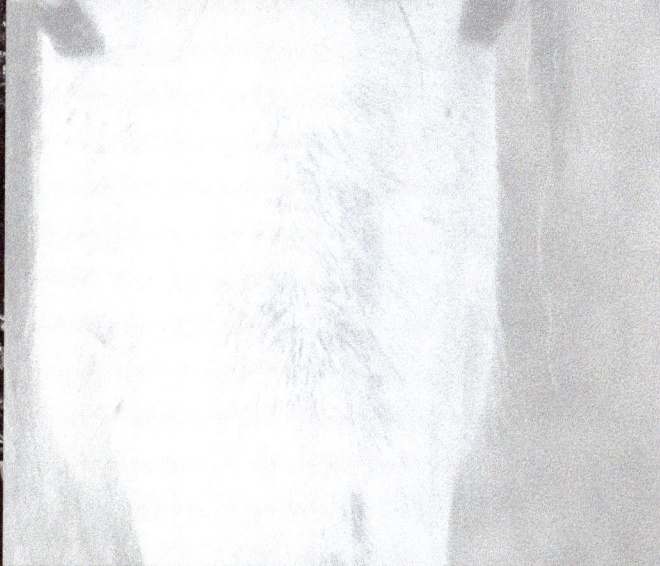

Chasing Horses
NOTES

2002 Stallion Copper

2002 Stallion Copper's band consists of:
2006 Mare Daisy
2011 Mare Esprit
2011 Mare Juniper
2013 Mare Faith
2014 Mare Grace
2020 Filly Belle

Stallion Copper had quite an interesting year! It is believed that he and Mystery were probably fighting around the time that Mystery died. We have seen the two posture with each other on several occasions. We will never know why exactly these two didn't get along, but it was clear they did NOT like each other!

At the beginning of 2020, Copper initially had his band that consisted of: Mares Daisy, Esprit, Juniper, Faith, and Democracy. In the spring of 2020, Faith gave birth to a filly named Belle and Democracy gave birth to a colt named Bart. Copper is the presumed sire of both.

When Mystery died in May, Copper had his band PLUS Mystery's band which consisted of: Mares Sundance, Cheyenne, Cedar, Raven, Eagle, Ember's Girl, Grace, along with Mystery's 2020 fillies: Birdie, Raven's Myst and Emery. YES! At one time this year, Copper's band consisted of 18 horses!!!

We knew this was not good for the then 18-year-old. Such a large band would make him the target of the younger bachelor stallions without a doubt!

Mare Ember's Girl and her 2020 Filly Emery along with Mare Eagle and her 2020 Filly Birdie were not so sure that Copper was the right band stallion for them.

The four briefly visited with Stallion Satellite. Ember's Girl and her filly even spent a couple days giving Stallion Trooper a shot at being a band stallion again. Eventually the foursome found a home with Stallion Red Face, but only after months of the four moving back and forth between Copper & Red Face.

Holding onto 14 horses proved to be equally as challenging for Copper as his original band and his new band did not seem to be getting along. His old band was usually a good distance away from where he was trying to hold his new band additions. This would eventually cost him Mare Democracy and their 2020 colt Bart. Copper lost the two to Bachelor Stallion Remington in July as well.

Maybe 12 horses would prove to be easier to handle?

Copper's band would be shaken up again as he would lose Mares Sundance, Cheyenne, Cedar & Raven along with Raven's 2020 filly, Raven's Myst to Mystery's son, Stallion Gunner.

Once all of his losses were cut, Copper would end up only gaining Mare Grace.

2006 Mare Daisy

2011 Mare Esprit

2011 Mare Juniper

2014 Mare Grace

2013 Mare Faith
gave birth to a filly
on March 15, 2020.

The filly was
given the name
Belle.

Chasing Horses
NOTES

2011 Stallion Flax

2011 Stallion Flax's Band consists of:
2006 Mare Dolly
2007 Mare Firefly
2007 Mare Smokie
2013 Mare Mischief
2014 Mare Kat
2018 Mare Patience
2019 Filly Amargo
2019 Filly Anuk
2019 Colt Anzar
2020 Filly Bird
2020 Colt Bokel
2020 Filly Bluff

Stallion Flax ended up having a pretty exciting year!

His year started with Mare Kat having another beautiful filly in May, followed by Mare Dolly having another adorable colt in June.

Flax's big news came in the fall of 2020 when he managed to take his half-brother Frontier's band! This would make Flax's band the largest he has ever held. His band now totals 13 horses! Time will tell if he is able to keep them!

One of the biggest highlights of the year came because of Covid. All captures were cancelled which meant we got to witness the changing band dynamics in ways we normally don't get to see. Mare Mischief and Filly Amargo became BFF's as Mare Kat welcomed another beautiful filly into the band. This gave Kat time to focus her attention on her new Filly Bird while Mischief became a mentor to Amargo.

We just could not get enough Mare Dolly's colts,
Anzar and Bokel, this year! Anzar stepped up and took
some lessons from his dad and seems to have learned a lot.
In his spare time, Anzar entertained his younger brother,
Bokel. We believe no one probably appreciated this more
than Mare Dolly!

As Kat is getting ready to have another baby in 2021, we are
seeing that her 2020 Filly Bird has shifted from being at
her side as often as she has been to hanging out with her older
sister Amargo and Mare Mischief.

We can't wait to see what 2021 holds for Flax and company!

2006 Mare Dolly gave birth to a colt in June of 2020. Stallion Flax is the presumed sire.

The colt was given the name Bokel.

2007 Mare Firefly gave birth to a filly in May of 2020. Stallion Frontier is the presumed sire.

The filly was given the name Bluff.

2007
Mare
Smokie

2018
Mare
Patience

2014 Mare Kat gave birth to a filly in May of 2020. Stallion Flax is the presumed sire.

The filly was given the name Bird.

2013
Mare
Mischief

2019
Filly
Amargo

2019 Filly Anuk

2019 Colt Anzar

Chasing Horses
NOTES

2005 Stallion Georgia's Boy

2005 Stallion Georgia's Boy's band
consists of:
1996 Mare Flicka
2002 Mare Shale
2010 Mare Whiskey
2014 Mare Vicki
2014 Mare Holly
2021 Filly Noelle

Georgia's Boy has remained pretty well hidden with his band since he became a band stallion again in July of 2019. It seems that seven months of bachelorhood has added to his wisdom. Georgia's Boy and his ladies have been observed by most at a distance through 2020.

Georgia's Boy welcomed the first new foal of 2021 on January 8th when Mare Holly gave birth to a filly named Noelle.

1996 Mare Flicka

This pretty lady deserves a page of her own! Flicka is currently the oldest horse in the entire Theodore Roosevelt National park herd!

This amazing mare turns 25 years old this year! She looks FANTASTIC!

Flicka has four offspring still living wild and free in Theodore Roosevelt National Park:
2000 Stallion Circus
2005 Stallion Coal
2007 Mare Maggie
2006 Mare Raven

2002
Mare
Shale

2010
Mare
Whiskey

2014
Mare
Vicki

2014 Mare Holly gave birth to the very first foal born in 2021 to the TRNP herd on January 8.

Her filly has been named Noelle.

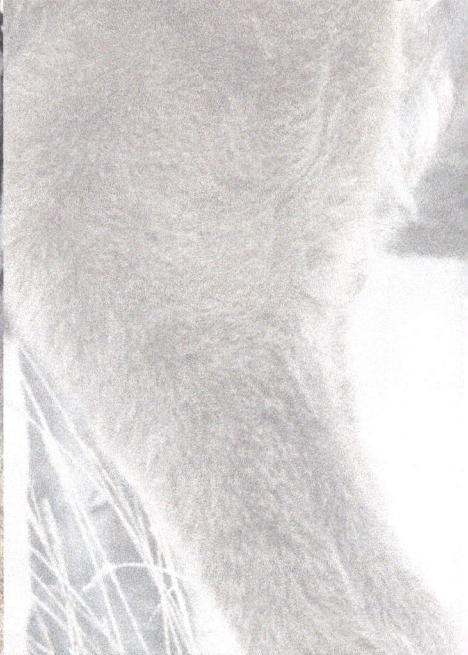

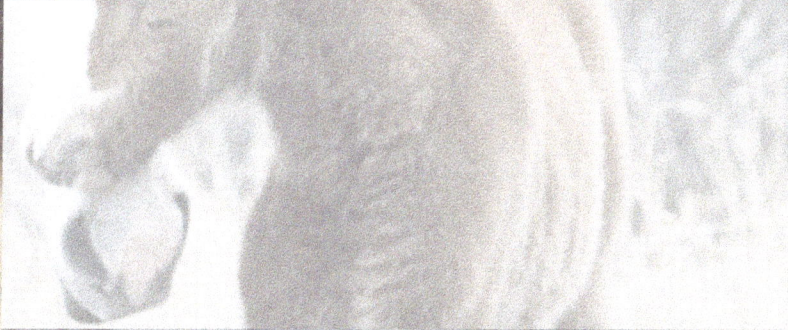

Chasing Horses
NOTES

2015 Stallion Grady

2015 Stallion Grady's band consists of:
2005 Mare Blondie
2005 Mare Twister
2014 Mare Quinn
2019 Colt Arcola
2020 Filly Bonnet

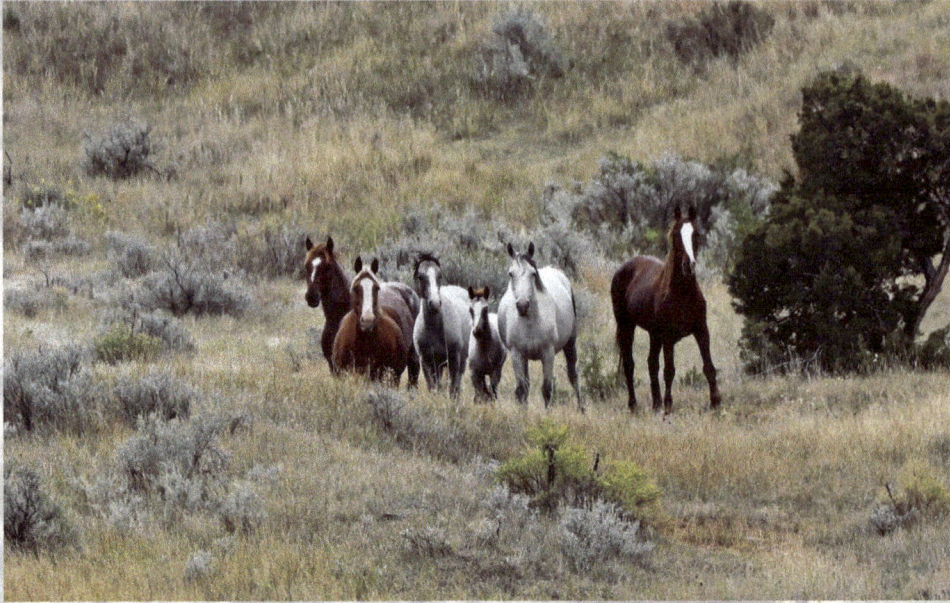

2015 Stallion Grady is currently the youngest band stallion we have in Theodore Roosevelt National Park.

In a series of weird events beginning in August of 2019, Grady successfully took control of the band from his half-brother Ranger in October of 2019. Stallion Ranger was never seen again.

Grady seems to be earning the respect of his ladies.

In July of 2020, Grady welcomed his first born when Mare Quinn gave birth to a filly that has been named Bonnet.

2005 Mare Blondie

2005 Mare Twister

2019 Colt Arcola

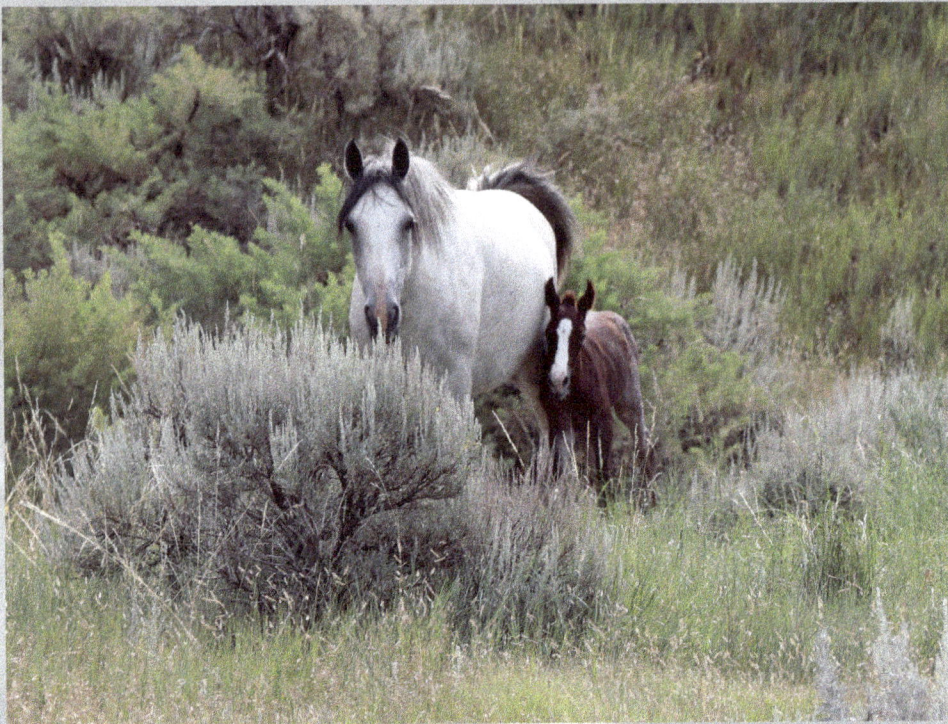

Quinn and Arcola shortly after his birth in 2019.

2019 Colt Arcola was Mare Quinn's first recorded birth.

His sire is unknown but is assumed to be either the late Stallion Gray Ghost or the late Stallion Ranger.

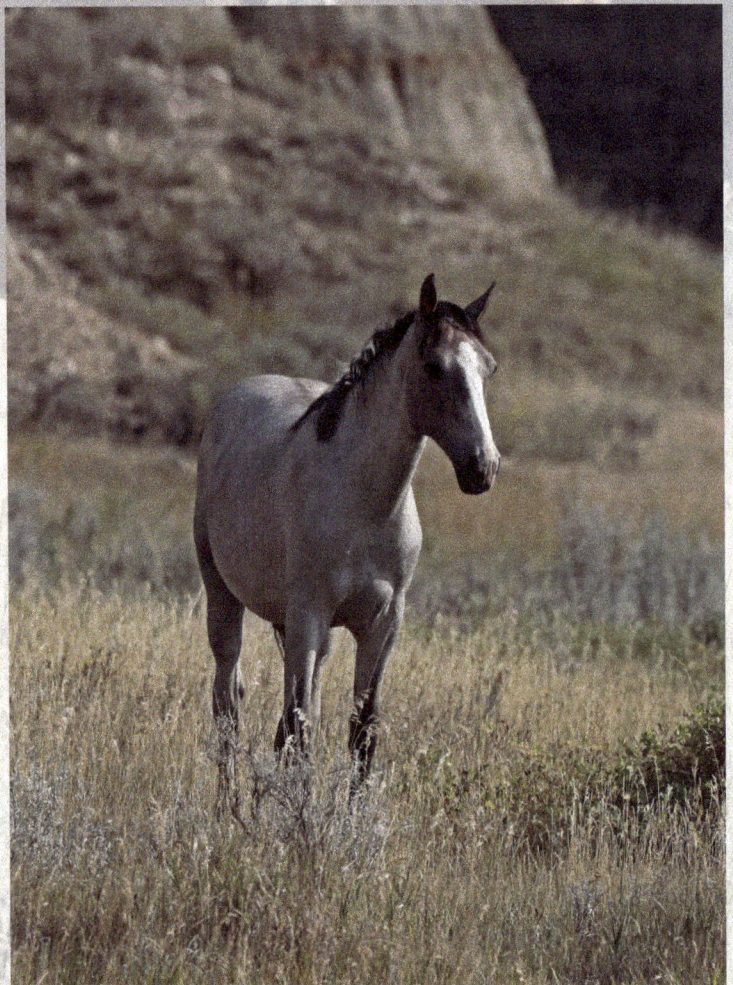

2014
Mare
Quinn

In July of 2020,
Mare Quinn &
Stallion Grady
welcomed a new filly
to the band.

The filly was
given the name
Bonnet.

Chasing Horses
NOTES

2013 Stallion Guardian

2013 Stallion Guardian's Band consists of:
2004 Mare Freckles
2020 Filly Katie

2013 Stallion Guardian has had an on-going feud with Stallion Half Moon for years now! The two seem to battle the most over 2004 Mare Freckles.

Freckles usually spends the fall/winter months with Half Moon and then the spring and summer months with Guardian.

In April of 2020, Freckles gave birth to a filly named Katie. Guardian is the presumed sire.

Time will tell if this young stallion is able to hold onto Freckles for the entire year and if he is able to add any other mares to his band in 2021.

2004 Mare Freckles gave birth to a filly on April 13, 2020. Stallion Guardian is the presumed sire.

The filly has been given the name Katie.

Chasing Horses
NOTES

2014 Stallion Gunner

2014 Stallion Gunner's Band consists of:
2005 Mare Sundance
2006 Mare Raven
2007 Mare Cedar
2020 Filly Raven's Myst

Last seen as part of this band,
but currently running alone:
2017 Mare Perdita
2019 Filly Anisak
2020 Filly Birch

2014 Stallion Gunner had a pretty interesting year.

Gunner won his first mare in the spring of 2019 after fighting it out with his former bachelor buddy Flash and eventually winning Mare Perdita and her then new filly Anisak. Gunner and Perdita welcomed a new filly to their band this year. Filly Birch rounded out this sweet little band creating a band of four in 2020.

The four seemed happy together and Gunner and Perdita were likened to a couple of teenagers.

When Gunner's father, Stallion Mystery, passed away, the mares scrambled to find their new "home". After spending some time with Stallion Copper, in July of 2020, Mares Sundance, Cheyenne, Cedar, Raven and Filly Raven's Myst joined Gunner's band. It was immediately apparent that Perdita was NOT happy with the new arrangement. In August, Mare Cheyenne passed away unexpectedly.

At times it seemed like the whole band was getting along better until December of 2020 when Gunner's band was spotted without Perdita and her kids. Perdita and the girls were spotted on the complete opposite end of the park from where Gunner is currently keeping his band.

Time will tell if Perdita, Anisak and Birch get picked up by another stallion or return to Gunner and his band. We have decided to add them under Gunner's band because that was the last band they belonged to. Stay tuned to our Facebook page for additional updates.

2005 Mare Sundance

2007 Mare Cedar

2006 Mare Raven
gave birth to a filly
on February 10, 2020.
Stallion Mystery is
the presumed sire.

The filly was given
the name
Raven's Myst.

2017 Mare Perdita

2017 Mare Perdita has an interesting story to tell! If only she would talk to us!

This young mare has proven to be quite the strong and independent one!

Perdita gave birth last year to a filly named Anisak. Her sire is unknown. She and her filly walked alone, with Perdita protecting her filly, as bachelor stallions Flash and Gunner fought daily for the young mare.

Flash was the initial winner of Perdita and Anisak. Within a few weeks, Gunner had managed to take Perdita and Anisak from him. Gunner kept his new little band well hidden, and in April, this little band welcomed Filly Birch.

After Gunner's father, Stallion Mystery died, after months of back and forth between the mares to different bands, Gunner ended up with the majority of his late father's band.

This did not sit well with Perdita and obviously upset their little family unit. Perdita and her kids were often found a distance away from Gunner and his new band. We did see them in December of 2020, and it appeared that the whole band was getting along better. Mare Sundance had very obviously replaced Perdita at Gunner's side.

By the end of December, Gunner's band was spotted without Perdita and her kids. A couple of weeks later, Perdita, Anisak & Birch were spotted on the complete opposite end of the park from Gunner and his band.

As we go to print, Perdita and her kids are still walking alone. Time will tell if she returns to Gunner or if she finds a new stallion to be with. Watch for updates on Perdita and her kids on our Facebook page.

2019 Filly Anisak

2020 Filly Birch

Chasing Horses
NOTES

2010 Stallion Half Moon

2010 Stallion Half Moon's Band
consists of:
2001 Mare Tanker
2004 Mare Rosie
2009 Mare Punkin
2011 Mare Sumac
2014 Mare Eclipse
2019 Colt Aloe
2020 Filly Bea
2020 Filly Star

Aside from the usual antics between Half Moon and Guardian, Half Moon had a pretty quiet year. Guardian once again took Freckles from Half Moon in the spring of 2020.

Mare Punkin had the first new foal of the year for this band on April 2, 2020. Mare Eclipse had her first recorded foal 20 days later. Sadly, Mare Rosie lost her baby this year.

We did catch Half Moon laying on his charms with several mares outside of his band this year. Sadly, he was not able to add any new mares to his band.

2001
Mare
Tanker

2004
Mare
Rosie

2011
Mare
Sumac

2009 Mare Punkin gave birth to a filly on April 2, 2020.

The filly was given the name Bea.

2014 Mare Eclipse gave birth to her first recorded foal, a filly, on April 20, 2020.

The filly was given the name Star.

2019 Colt Aloe

Chasing Horses
NOTES

2014 Stallion Maverick

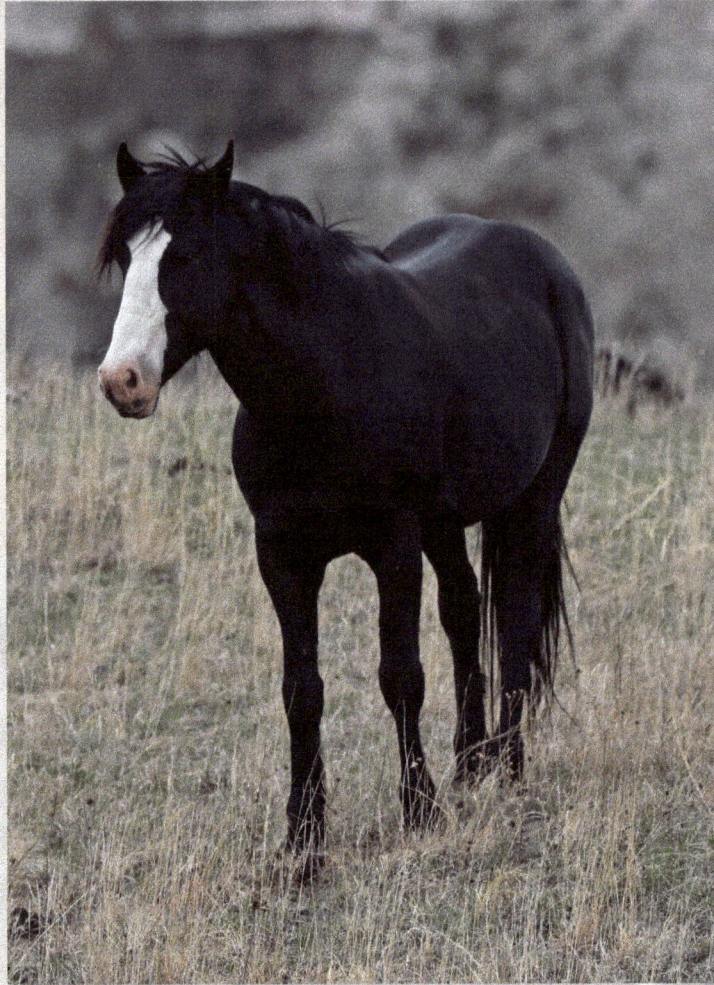

2014 Stallion Maverick's Band
consists of:
2016 Mare Patches
2017 Mare Aurora
2020 Filly Bluegrass

2014 Stallion Maverick spent 2020 getting the hang of this band stallion thing. Maverick spent 2019 fighting with Stallion Brutus for his band. In September of 2019, Maverick had successfully taken the entire band from the older stallion.

2021 may prove to be Stallion Brutus's year! In an upsetting turn of events for Maverick, Brutus ended up with the majority of his band back as 2021 rang in!

Maverick was left with the youngest of his original band: Mare Patches, Mare Aurora and their 2020 Filly Bluegrass. Time will tell what the next moves will be for this young stallion and his band.

While we were happy to see Mare Aurora welcome her first baby to the band, sadly, Mare Patches lost her first baby in May of 2020.

Here is hoping that 2021 is better for this band!

2016 Mare Patches

2017 Mare Aurora gave birth to her first foal on June 1, 2020. Stallion Maverick is the presumed sire of her filly.

The filly was given the name Bluegrass.

2010 Stallion Ollie Jr.

2010 Stallion Ollie Jr.'s Band consists of:
1999 Mare Stormy
2007 Mare Autumn
2007 Mare Sapphire
2019 Colt Applewood
2019 Filly Aqua
2020 Filly Jewel
2020 Filly Pixie
2020 Filly Bess

2010 Stallion Ollie Jr. continued to add to his growing band this year as all three of his mares foaled again.

Mare Sapphire starting the foaling party on June 2, 2020 when she gave birth to a filly that was named Jewel. Mare Stormy foaled two days after Sapphire. She too had a filly that was named Pixie. Mare Autumn Foaled on August 8, 2020 giving birth to a filly that was named Bess.

Ollie Jr. was another neat band to watch this year. Covid allowed us to watch the changing dynamics within the bands especially when there were both yearlings and new foals in the band. Ollie Jr.'s 2019 Colt Applewood spent 2020 very clearly learning from his dad. Applewood became a secondary protector of their band.

1999 Mare Stormy gave birth to a filly in June.

The filly was given the name Pixie.

2007 Mare Autumn gave birth to a filly in August.

The filly was given the name Bess.

2007 Mare Sapphire gave birth to a filly in June.

The filly was given the name Jewel.

2019
Filly
Aqua

2019
Colt
Applewood

Chasing Horses
NOTES

2014 Stallion Remington

2014 Stallion Remington's Band consists of:

2013 Mare Democracy
2020 Colt Bart

2014 Stallion Remington became a band stallion when he managed
to take Mare Democracy and her 2020 Colt Bart from Stallion Copper
in July.

Copper had been preoccupied with his enormous band at the
time, so it is not surprising that he lost Democracy.

Remington has held mares for a very short time only to lose them
almost as soon as he gained them. It looks like Democracy is settling
in with him.

2013 Mare Democracy gave birth to a colt on March 22, 2020.

The colt was given the name Bart.
Stallion Copper is the presumed sire.

Chasing Horses
NOTES

2001 Stallion Red Face

2001 Stallion Red Face's Band
consists of:
1999 Mare Frosty
2000 Mare Flame
2003 Mare Pretty Girl
2006 Mare Ember's Girl
2010 Mare Lakota
2013 Mare Eagle
2014 Mare Emmylou
2019 Filly Ardena
2020 Colt Banty
2020 Filly Birdie
2020 Filly Emery
2020 Filly Little Mo

2001 Stallion Red Face ended up having a pretty eventful year.

Mare Frosty gave birth to one of the only colts born to this herd in 2020. Frosty gave birth to Colt Banty on March 18, 2020. Mare Flame gave birth to the last foal of 2020. Flame gave birth to Filly Little Mo on October 1, 2020.

Sadly, 2002 Mare Molly passed away in September of 2020. It is believed that she was the victim of an unfortunate accident that took her life.

The big news for this band came about because of the death of Stallion Mystery.

Mare Ember's Girl and Mare Eagle did not seem interested in following along with the rest of Mystery's mares. It did take them a short while to make a solid decision. While they were waiting to make a final decision, they did move back and forth between Stallion Copper's band and Stallion Red Face's band. In the end, Red Face ended up adding Mare Ember's Girl, her filly Emery, Mare Eagle and her filly Birdie to his band. Not to bad for a stallion who turns 20 years old this year!

1999 Mare Frosty gave birth to a colt in March.

The colt was given the name Banty.

2000 Mare Flame gave birth to the final 2020 baby for this herd in October.

The filly was given the name Little Mo.

2003 Mare Pretty Girl

2010 Mare Lakota

2006 Mare
Ember's Girl
gave birth to a filly
on April 12, 2020.

The filly was
given the name
Emery.
Stallion Mystery
is the presumed sire.

2013 Mare Eagle
gave birth to a filly
on March 21, 2020.

The filly was given
the name
Birdie.
Stallion Mystery is
the presumed sire.

2014 Mare Emmylou

2019 Filly Ardena

Chasing Horses

NOTES

2001 Stallion Satellite

2001 Stallion Satellite's Band
consists of:
1998 Mare Lightening
2007 Mare Crow
2016 Mare Minnie
2019 Filly Almanac
2020 Filly Little Bear

2001 Stallion Satellite seemed to make his rounds this year letting the younger stallions know that age is just a number! We caught glimpses of him letting Gunner know he felt he was too close to his band. We also have seen him trying to put Flax in his place as well.

Of course, Satellite is a lover above all else, so he is always looking to woo nearby mares!

Satellite had Mare Ember's Girl and Mare Eagle, along with their fillies for a brief moment when Stallion Mystery died.

Mare Crow gave birth to a beautiful filly named Little Bear on March 27th. Sadly, Mare Lightening lost her foal this year for unknown reasons.

1998 Mare Lightening

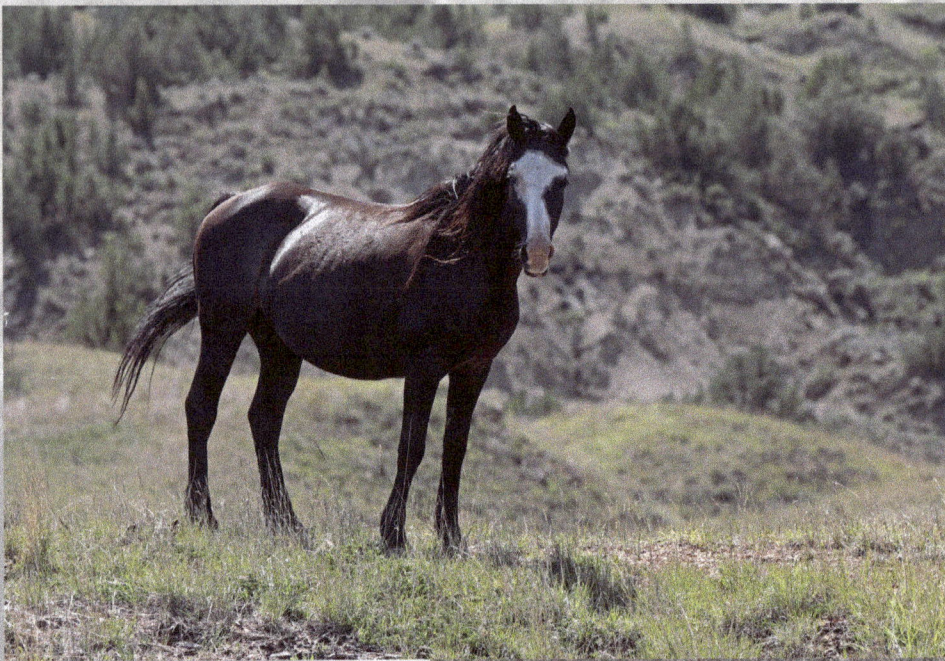

2007 Mare Crow gave birth to a filly in March.

The filly was given the name Little Bear.

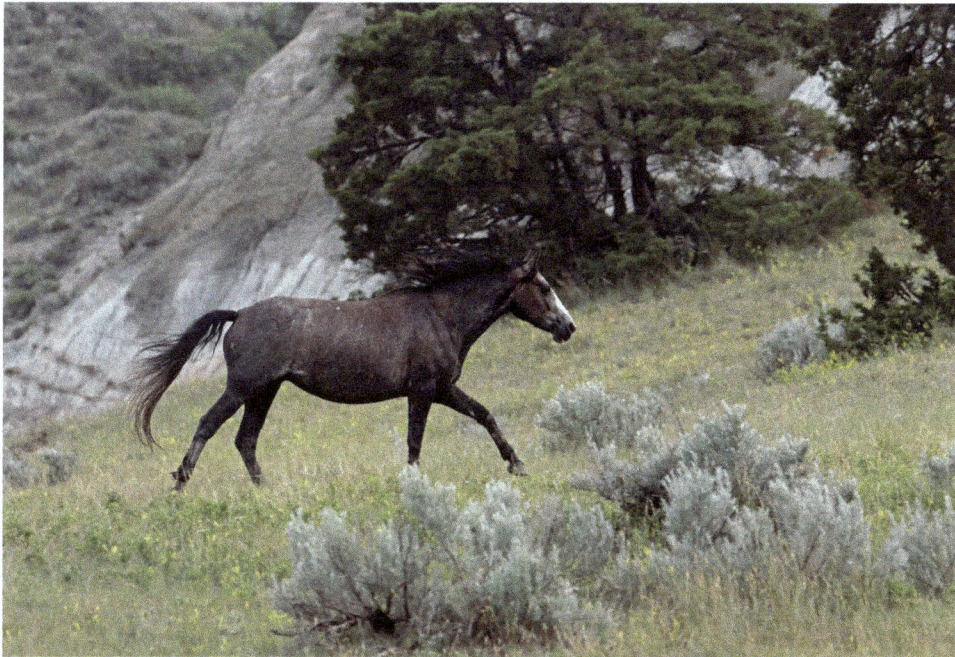

2016
Mare
Minnie

Minnie
&
Almanac

2019
Filly
Almanac

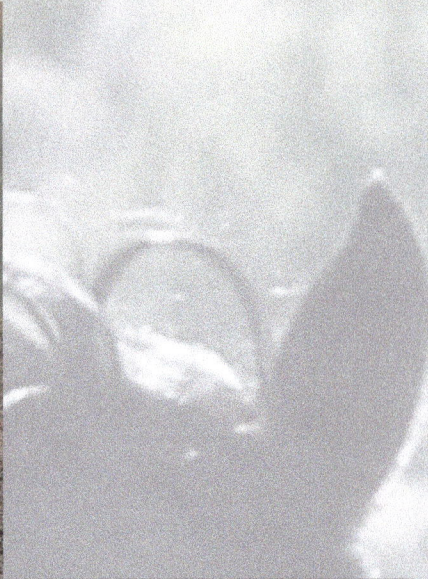

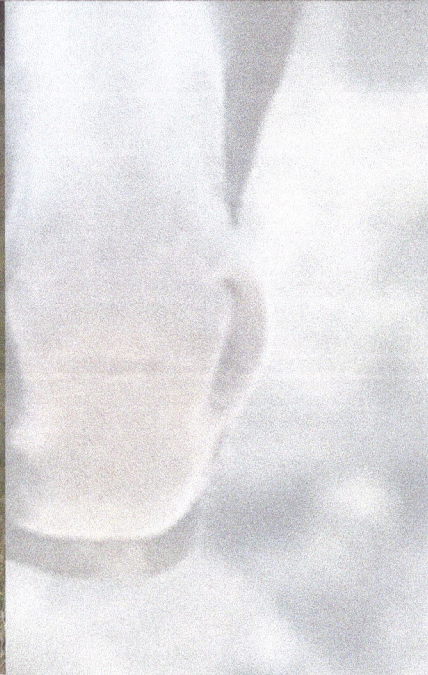

Chasing Horses
NOTES

2004 Stallion Sidekick

2004 Stallion Sidekick's Band
consists of:
2001 Mare Bella
2001 Mare Snip's Gray
2005 Mare Mist
2006 Mare Escape
2006 Mare River
2010 Mare Maiden
2014 Mare Valentina
2020 Filly Misty Blue
2020 Filly Bayou
2020 Filly Annabella

2001 Stallion Sidekick had an eventful year welcoming 3 new foals to his band in 2020!

Mare Mist kicked things off when she gave birth to a filly that was named Misty Blue on March 16th. Mare River followed, having another filly on March 26th that was named Bayou. Filly Annabella was the last of the live births for this band in 2020. She was born to Mare Bella April 3rd. Sadly, it is believed that Mare Maiden lost her baby this year for unknown reasons.

Sidekick and Snip's Gray's daughter, Valentina, has been seen with other bands occasionally. This may be a sign that after 5 years, she may be ready to leave her natal band! She does always end up back with her family, so time will tell how this plays out.

Sidekick is a strong stallion that does not get challenged too often. It was interesting to watch him this year with young bachelor stallion Illinois. Their interactions suggested that Sidekick cut Illinois some slack and entertained him in a teaching manner.

These horses are amazing!

2001 Mare Bella gave
birth to a filly in April.

The filly was
given the name
Annabella.

2001
Mare
Snip's Gray

2014
Mare
Valentina

2005
Mare Mist
gave birth to
a filly in March.

The filly was
given the name
Misty Blue.

2006 Mare Escape

2010 Mare Maiden

2006 Mare River
gave birth to a
filly in March.

The filly was
given the name
Bayou.

Chasing Horses
NOTES

2010 Stallion Teton

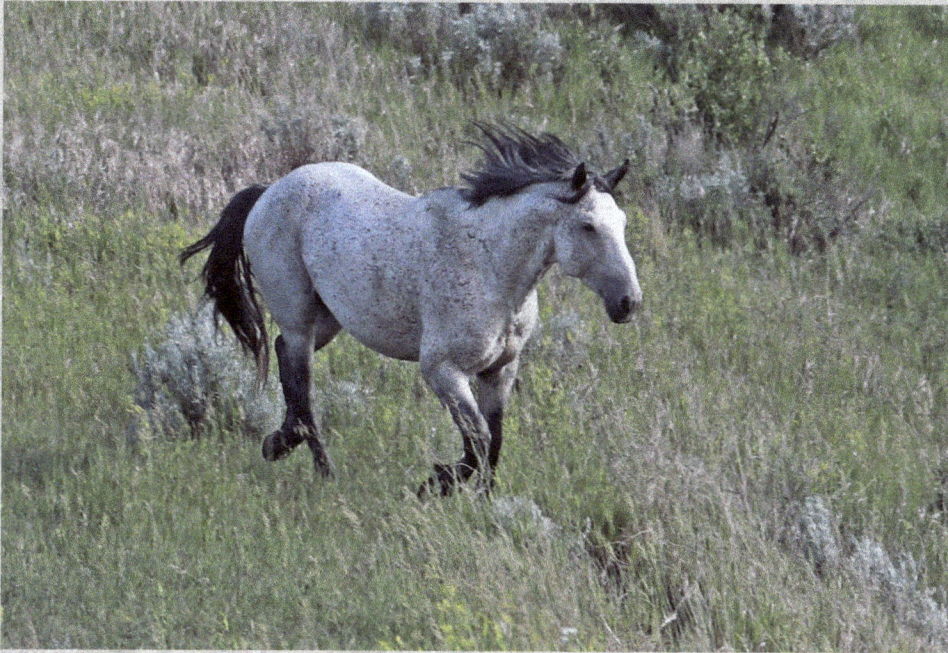

2010 Stallion Teton's Band consists of:
2006 Mare Ruby
2009 Mare Goblin
2010 Mare Teepee
2011 Mare Indian Paint Brush
2014 Mare June
2019 Colt Alluvium
2019 Colt Apex
2019 Filly Archer
2020 Filly Bee
2020 Filly Shayna
2020 Filly Berkleigh
2020 Colt Bonanza

2010 Stallion Teton continued to grow his band in 2020 as 4 of his 5 mares gave birth!

Indian Paint Brush started the new baby party when she gave birth to the first new baby for this band on April 4, 2020. She had a filly that was given the name Bee. Mare June was next with another filly that was given the name Shayna on April 12, 2020. Goblin was next with another filly that was born on April 20, 2020. Mare Ruby was the last to add to the new babies when she gave birth to a colt on July 14, 2020. He was given the name Bonanza.

Sadly, Mare TeePee lost her baby in 2020 for unknown reasons. Teton and his band are usually found at the entrance to the park.

2006 Mare Ruby
gave birth to a colt
in July.

The colt was
given the name
Bonanza.

2010 Mare Teepee

2019 Filly Archer

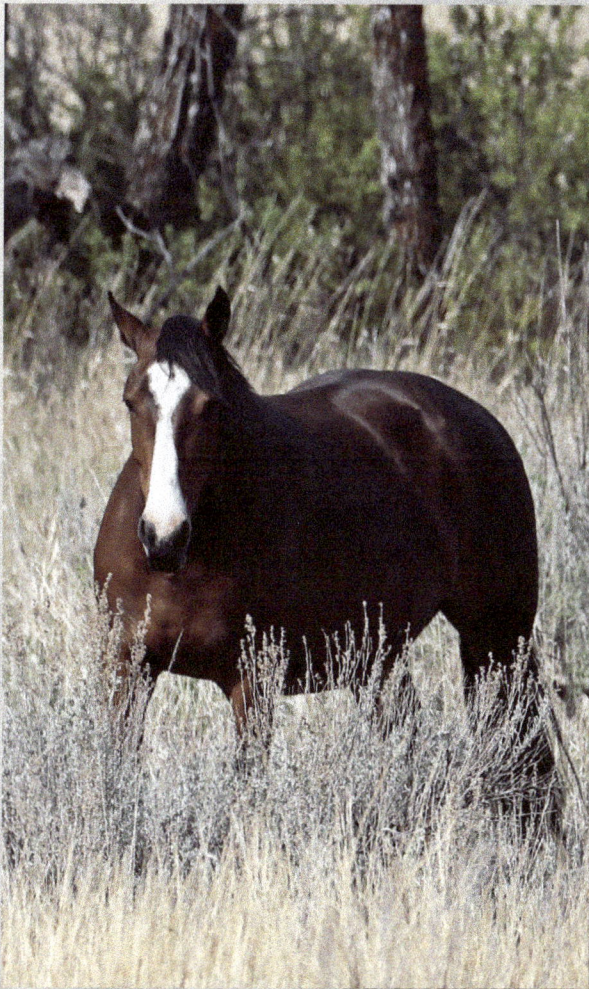

2011 Mare Indian Paint Brush gave birth to a filly in April.

The filly was given the name Bee.

2014 Mare June gave birth to a filly in April.

The filly was given the name Shayna.

2019 Colt
Alluvium

2019 Colt Apex

Chasing Horses
NOTES

2013 Stallion Trooper

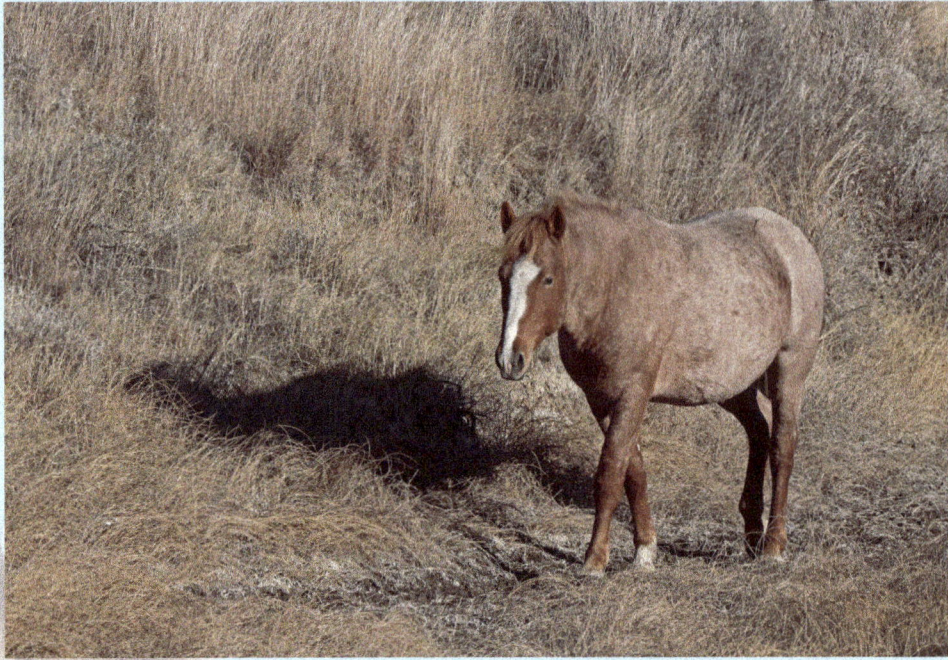

2013 Stallion Trooper had a pretty eventful year!

He had been hanging out with his new bachelor buddies, Flash & Brutus since the spring of 2020.

In July, he managed to take Mare Ember's Girl and her Filly Emery for a couple of days while they were shuffling from band to band looking for a new home.

We witnessed the determined young bachelor challenging stallions Copper, Satellite, Remington, Ollie Jr., & Gunner.

In the fall of 2020, Trooper once again gained himself a mare when he managed to get 2007 Mare Maddie from Stallion Maverick.

Time will tell if he is able to hold onto Maddie and/or add to his band in 2021.

2007
Mare
Maddie

Chasing Horses
NOTES

2011 Stallion Wild Rye

2011 Stallion Wild Rye's Band
consists of:
2001 Mare Trouble's Girl
2004 Mare Little Gray
2014 Mare Lorena
2014 Mare Paige
2019 Colt Anthem
2020 Filly Lorelye
2020 Filly Pippi
2020 Colt Blazo

2011 Stallion Wild Rye welcomed three new members to his band in 2020!

Mare Lorena kicked off the baby boom for the band when she had her first ever foal on March 21, 2020. She is a proud mom and also stayed close to Mare Little Gray for guidance. Lorena's filly was named Lorelye. Little Gray also had a filly on April 16, 2020 that was named Pippi. Mare Trouble's Girl gave birth to the only colt born to the band this year on May 11, 2020.

Mare Trouble's Girl has been seen moving back and forth between Stallion Grady's band and Wild Rye's band. She has her two boys with her. She is an older mare and on the thin side. We have listed her with this band, but she can be seen with either band. She has been seen alone with her two boys at times as well.

2014
Mare
Paige

2001 Mare Trouble's Girl gave birth to a colt in May.

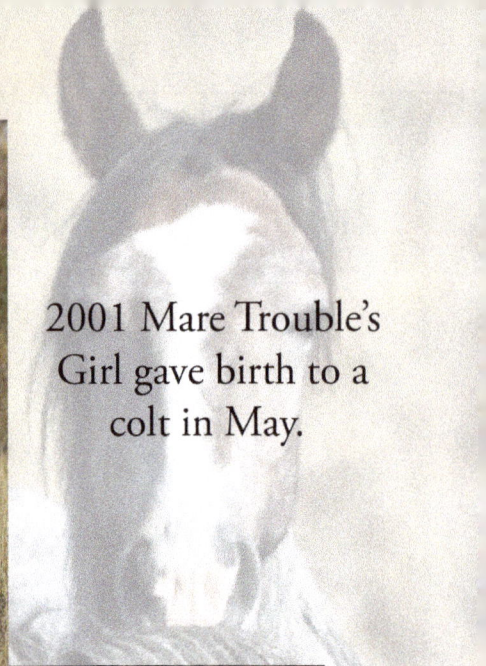

He was given the name Blazo.

2019 Colt Anthem

2014 Mare Lorena
gave birth to a filly
in March.

2004 Mare Little Gray
gave birth to a filly
in April.

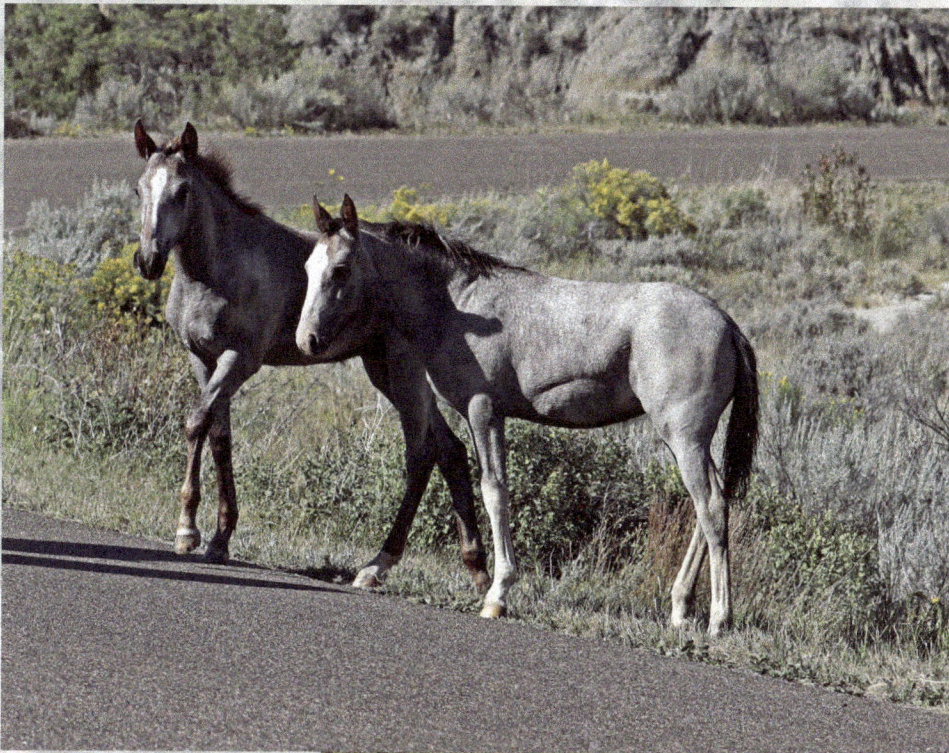

Lorena's filly (L) was given the name Lorelye.

Little Gray's filly (R) was given the name Pippi.

Chasing Horses
NOTES

2014 Stallion Xander

2014 Stallion Xander's Band
consists of:
2001 Mare Pale Lady
2004 Mare Winter
2005 Mare Spotted Blue
2007 Mare Angel
2010 Mare Cowgirl
2014 Mare Taylor
2019 Colt Amite
2020 Filly Blue Angel
2020 Colt Boomer

And the winner of the craziest 2020 for the TRNP herd is……

(Envelope please!)

2014 Stallion Xander!

What a year this young stallion and his entire band had!

You may remember that Xander's sire, Stallion Thunder Cloud, tried for YEARS to kick Xander out of his band with no luck! That is because Xander's mom, Mare Cowgirl, fought with Thunder every time he tried.

In 2019, Thunder was FINALLY successful in kicking Xander out of his band. Xander spent the year as a bachelor and was really never too far from his natal band.

Once spring of 2020 came, Xander got more aggressive about taking his father's band. 2001 Stallion Thunder was amazing fighting his son off until April of 2020. Xander somehow managed to get the band from his father. This left an injured Thunder on his own. At times, Thunder was found near the band. Xander would quickly chase him away.

Thunder walked alone for a bit in the spring but by summer, he was found on the outskirts of the band again. He has remained close to the band since. Xander does occasionally let him know if he is too close to the band. In the last couple months of 2020, Cowgirl was seen keeping Thunder company. The two were often found off to the side together, ironically, very similar to what we seen with Cowgirl and Xander before he was successfully kicked out of the band in 2019.

Time will tell how the #1 soap opera storyline of this herd plays out!

In other news:
Mare Angel gave birth to a filly that was named Blue Angel on March 3, 2020. Mare Strawberry gave birth to everyone's favorite colt – Boomer, on May 21, 2020. Sadly, Mare Taylor's filly that was named Bedrock failed to thrive and died shortly after her birth on or around April 4, 2020.

Another huge loss to this band was the death of Mare Strawberry in November of 2020. Her Colt Boomer remains with his natal band and can usually be found close to his brother, 2019 Colt Amite.

2001
Mare
Pale
Lady

2004 Mare Winter

2005
Mare
Spotted
Blue

2010
Mare
Cowgirl

2014
Mare
Taylor

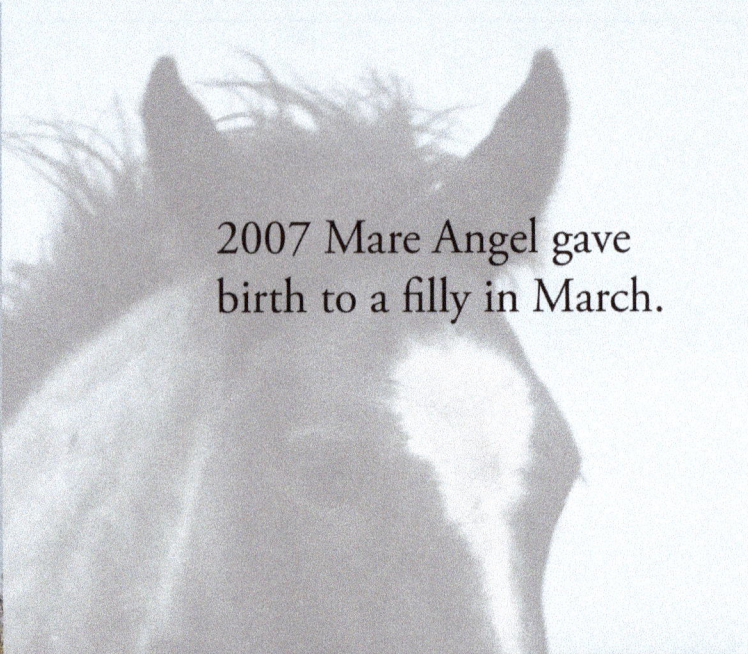

2007 Mare Angel gave
birth to a filly in March.

The filly was
given the name
Blue Angel.
Stallion Thunder Cloud
is her presumed sire.

2019 Colt Amite was born to the late Mare Strawberry. Since her death, he has remained with his natal band and has been looking after his younger brother Boomer.

2020 Colt Boomer is the last foal that the late Mare Strawberry would have. This beautiful boy with two blue eyes has captured the hearts of many!

Chasing Horses
NOTES

Bachelor Stallions

2000 Stallion Circus

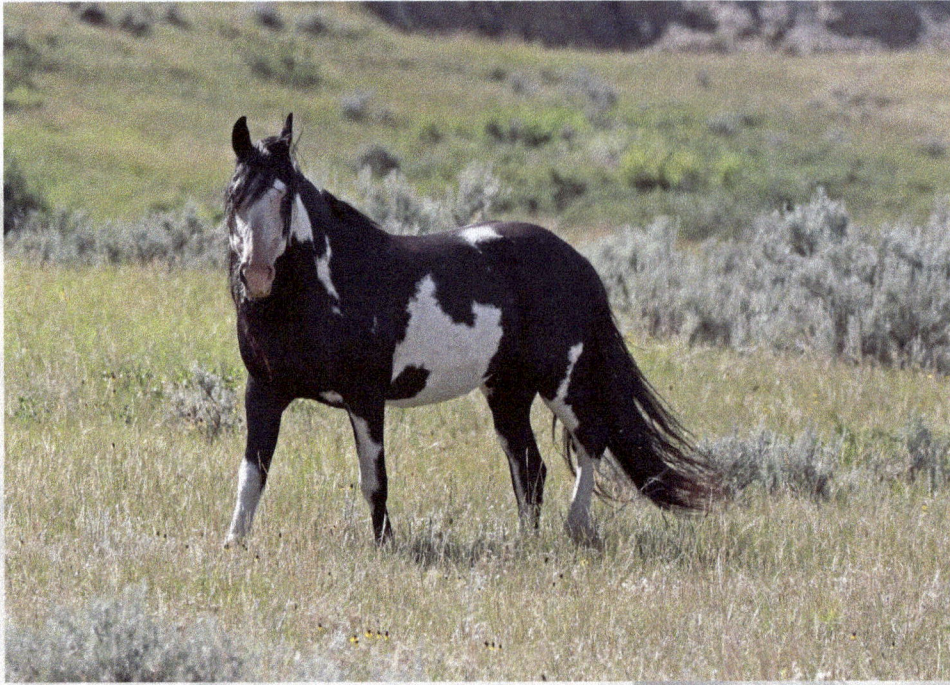

2000 Stallion Circus spends most of his time by himself in the Petrified forest area of Theodore Roosevelt National Park. When he does come into the main part of the park, things usually get shaken up a bit!

Circus came into the main part of the park in during the summer of 2020. He spent a lot of time confronting Stallion Frontier. He also made his rounds and postured with stallions Maverick and Flax.

Circus is the oldest stallion currently living in Theodore Roosevelt National Park. His mother, Mare Flicka, is the oldest horse in this herd.

2001 Stallion Thunder Cloud

2001 Stallion Thunder Cloud became a bachelor in April of 2020 when he lost his band to his son Xander.

Thunder is still seen close to the band. At times, he appears to actually be part of the band. Time will tell if he is able to take his band back from his son.

2004 Stallion Cloud

2004 Stallion Cloud and 2014 Stallion Nicols have been bachelor buddies since Cloud lost his band to Flax in June of 2019.

Cloud and his band were once one of the most seen/photographed horses in the park. This past year he has been almost as elusive as Circus.

Nicols has been seen visiting bachelor stallions Yoakum, Cagney and Illinois at times. He always seems to end up back with his BFF Cloud.

2014 Stallion Nicols

2014
Stallion
Flash

2014 Stallion Flash spent most of 2020 as a bachelor stallion. He was part of the bachelor trio that included stallions Brutus and Trooper. Brutus and Trooper have since gained some mares. Flash was able to take Mare Patches from Stallion Maverick briefly in July. She made her way back to Maverick within a few days.

It is easy to see that Flash is pretty intent on gaining some mares of his own. We will see what 2021 brings for this young stallion.

2012 Stallion Frontier

2012 Stallion Frontier decided for unknown reasons to move his band out from the middle of the park where they were far away from the other bands at the beginning of 2020.

Frontier seemed to be trying to flex his muscles as we witnessed him sparring with many different stallions through the year. Frontier also developed the bad habit of leaving his mares while he went out to fight with the other boys.

That may very well be how he lost his entire band to his older brother Flax in the fall of 2020. Frontier walked with Cloud and Nicols for a brief moment and has since only been seen walking alone but covering a good amount of ground. We will see if he challenges his older brother for his former band or what is next for this young stallion

Frontier and his band in the summer of 2020

2014
Stallion
Yoakum

2014 Stallion Yoakum found a new bachelor buddy when Illinois was kicked out of his natal band in 2019. In the spring of 2020, Yoakum's full brother Cagney was kicked out of his natal band by Stallion Frontier. Cagney turned the bachelor duo into a trio. The three have been seen giving Wild Rye, Flax and Grady a hard time. We will see what 2021 brings for these young stallions.

2016 Stallion Illinois

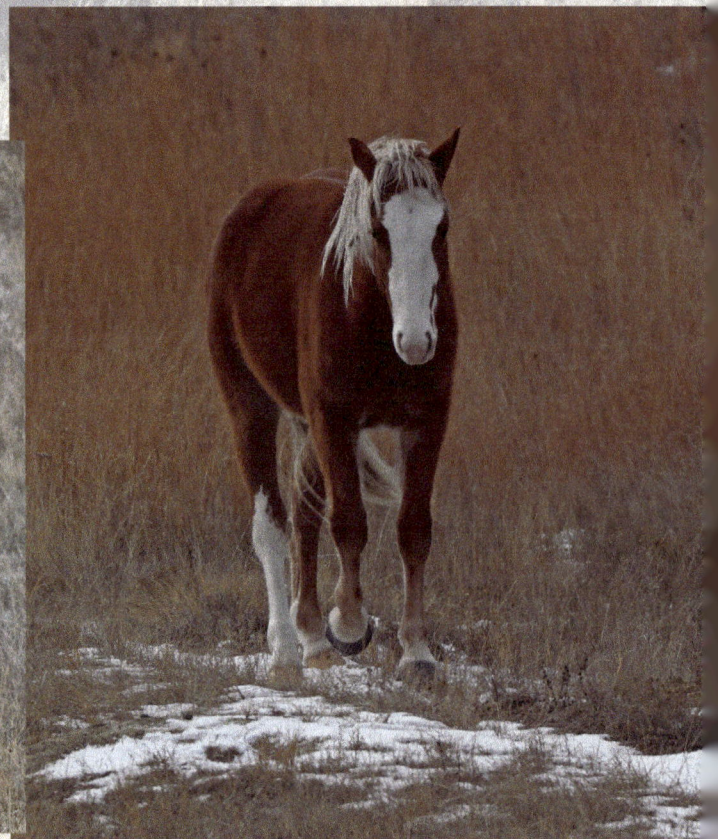

2018 Stallion Cagney

Chasing Horses
NOTES

Chasing Horses
NOTES

Forever Wild & Free

"It is the secret of the world that all things subsist and do not die, but retire a little from sight and afterwards return again."

~Ralph Waldo Emerson

Stallion Ranger

2013-2019

October of 2019 was the last time that we saw 2013 Stallion Ranger alive.

This seemingly healthy young stallion seemed to be settling in with the band he took from Stallion Gray Ghost the year before. In August of 2019, his half brother and former bachelor buddy Grady came calling and took the band from Ranger.

Ranger was stilling hanging out in the area and eventually Stallion Illinois joined him.

In October, Illinois was found wandering the park and eventually found Yoakum.

Ranger was never seen alive again.

We watched this young stallion get kicked out of his natal band and followed his journey to gaining his first band. We looked forward to watching him continue to learn and grow.

As beautiful as these horses are living wild and free, each loss takes a piece of our heart. Ranger took a huge chunk that is for sure!

Mare Quinn gave birth to a colt in 2019 named Arcola. The sire is unknown and only DNA will tell for sure. There is a good chance that Ranger could be Arcola's father.

Rest in Peace Ranger. Your life ended way too soon!

Mare Ginger

2005-2020

The first loss we had in 2020 was the beautiful Mare Ginger. She was part of Stallion Mystery's band. Little did we know in January that she was just the beginning of the losses that band would face in 2020.

Ginger died while she was giving birth. Something that is becoming all too common within this herd.

Mare Whiskey, who is currently in Stallion Georgia's Boys band, is Ginger's only offspring still in the park today. The late Stallion Gray Ghost is Whiskey's father.

Rest in Peace Ginger! Your beauty is missed!

Mare Cheyenne

2006-2020

In February of 2020, Mare Cheyenne lost her foal again this year. In August of 2020, she would join Stallion Mystery's every growing eternal herd as we found that she died for unknown reasons.

Cheyenne was a stunning mare! After Mystery died, she joined the other mares as they searched for a new home. After months of back and forth, they finally settled in with Mystery's son, Stallion Gunner.

We noticed in August that she was missing from the band. Her body was found, but her cause of death is unknown.

Cheyenne's last live foal was born in 2016. She and Mystery had a filly named Pocahontas. She was removed and sold.

Cheyenne's only offspring still in the park is Mare Sumac, who is currently in Stallion Half Moon's band. The late Stallion Mystery is her father.

Rest in Peace Cheyenne. You are missed!

Mare Molly

2002-2020

Mare Molly also passed away in September of 2020. She appears to have fallen in what we can only assume was an accident.

Molly was a long-time member of Stallion Red Face's band. Her last baby, 2014 Mare Opal, is her only offspring still living in the park. Red Face is Opal's sire. Opal is currently in Stallion Arrowhead's band.

Molly was a beautiful and very unique mare.

Mare Flame foaled in October, shortly after Molly passed away. Her filly was given the name Little Mo as a nod to Flame's long-time buddy.

Rest in Peace Molly. We feel your absence every time we sit with your band.

Mare Strawberry

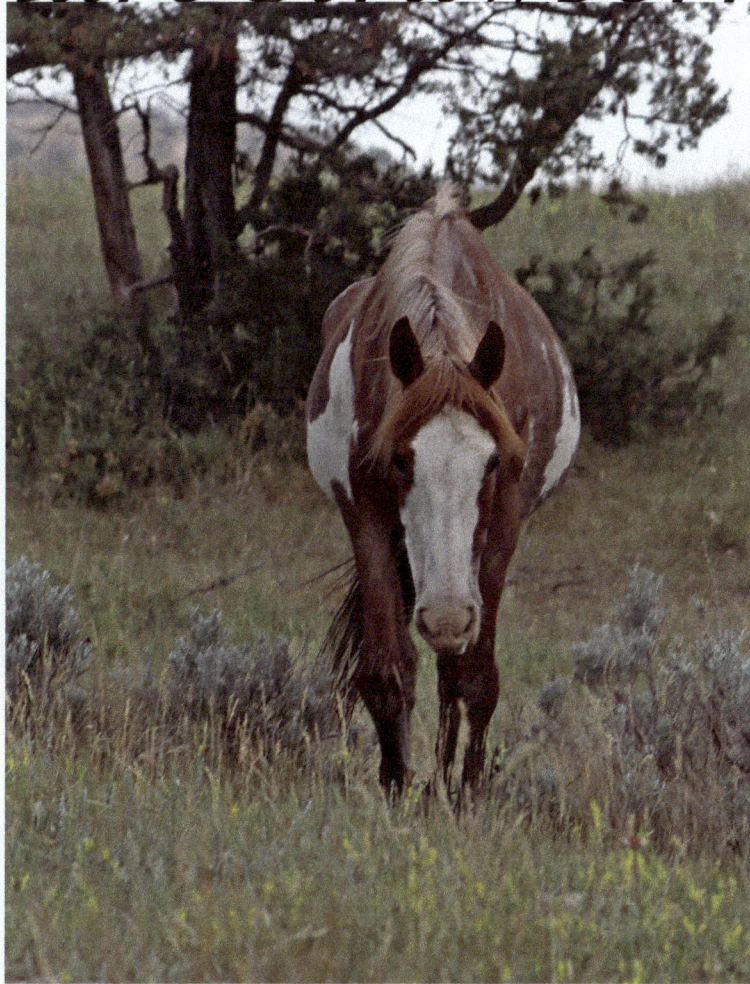

2000-2020

In November 2020 let us know that it wasn't quite done with us yet as we learned of the death of our beautiful Mare Strawberry.

Strawberry had been acting odd for weeks. It is believed that she was not able to keep up with her band. She and her 2020 Colt Boomer were found with several different bands for short amounts of time presumably until they could make their way back to their band.

The reason for Strawberry's death is unknown, but she leaves behind her orphaned Colt Boomer, who was born in May of 2020. Strawberry's 2019 Colt Amite is currently looking after his brother Boomer. They are both still with their natal band.

Mare Paisley is Strawberry's only other offspring still living in the park.

Rest in Peace Strawberry. Your spirit lives on in your children for sure!

Stallion Mystery

2004-2020

May of 2020 would bring news that would shake up all of us that love and follow these horses and the herd itself.

It was reported at the end of May that Stallion Mystery was missing. Even more disturbing was that Stallion Copper had Mastery's entire band. Mystery and Copper made no secret of their feelings for each other. They simply did not get along. While we never experienced any full-on fights between the two, there was always a lot of posturing and testosterone flying around when the two crossed paths.

We headed out to the park with a few others to look for our beloved missing stallion. We got to the park and found Copper's band. He was holding all of Mystery's band. All I could do was stand there and cry. There was no way Mystery was alive. Even if he was injured, he would not be too far away from his band. My husband tried to give me some encouraging words, but my heart knew we lost this amazing stallion.

Our friends that were out searching with us called us a few hours later to say that they found his body. While we will never know what happened for sure, he appeared to have fallen. This does not necessarily indicate that he fell as a result of fighting with Copper. The terrain of the badlands is rugged, hence the name. Also, there is a great detail of deterioration in the landscape. Any of these or any number of other reasons could have caused his death. The truth is, we will never know anymore than we lost one amazing stallion at the end of May.

My husband laughed at me often in our early visits to the park. We would see a group of horses and I would excitedly say, "Oh he's one of my favorites!" My husband started to believe that every horse was my favorite. That prompted me to think about who actually was my favorite?

My answer: Mystery.

He may look big in some of the photos we have shared. The truth is he was a smaller horse with a big attitude! He was a bad ass – that is always my best description of him. We witnessed him defending his band many times. He never waited for a stallion to approach him – he met challenges head on. We also got to witness the softer side if him. The stallion who loved his mares and made sure that even the newest mares in his band, like Eagle and Grace, got some of his time and attention. There were also deep levels of trust between him and his mares that was easily seen.

Nothing compared to watching this beautiful black stallion glide through the terrain of the badlands, never skipping a beat!

I could inject any series of adjectives here. Really all I can say is that being in his presence was simply amazing. We were blessed to share a few brief moments in this incredible stallion's life.

When we say his death sent shock waves through the park, that is not an exaggeration. It is interesting to see how one life impacts so many others.

At the time of his death, Mystery's band consisted of the following:
Mare Sundance
Mare Cheyenne
Mare Ember's Girl
Mare Raven
Mare Cedar
Mare Eagle
Mare Grace
2020 Filly Birdie
2020 Filly Raven's Myst
2020 Filly Emery

The sadness and confusion within this group of horses was apparent. We have no doubt they were mourning and that some are still mourning the loss of their great stallion.

Copper initially had the group. Mare Ember's Girl and Eagle, along with their fillies spent the first few weeks separating from the rest of the group. They were seen with Stallion Satellite, Stallion Red Face, Stallion Trooper and then back to Stallion Copper again. They finally started bouncing back and forth between Copper & Red Face. By fall, Red Face seemed to be their choice.

Mares Sundance, Cheyenne, Cedar, Raven and Raven's filly, Raven's Myst, stayed with Copper until July when this group was unexpectedly found with Mystery's son, Stallion Gunner.

This is a humorous point because there are some stallions that seem to have a "type" of mare in the make up of their bands. Mystery seemed to have a type. When those girls moved to his look-alike son's band, I couldn't help but wonder if we had it wrong all these years? Maybe the mares were the ones that actually had a type?

Mare Grace has remained with Stallion Copper in spite of everyone else's shuffling around.

Mare Cheyenne joined Mare Ginger and Stallion Mystery in September when she died unexpectedly. I took a moment when Cheyenne died to ask Mystery to quit calling his mares to his eternal herd!

As of this printing, Ember's Girl and her filly Emery along with Eagle and her filly Birdie remain with Stallion Red Face and seem to be getting along with the band. Sundance, Cedar, Raven and her filly Raven's Myst, remain with Mystery's son Gunner. Mare Grace has never left Copper's band since Mystery died.

Ember's Girl, Raven and Eagle all appear to be pregnant so we should see the last three of Mystery's babies born this spring.

Each one of these pages in this memorial section has felt like a final goodbye. They have been painful to write as I agonized over finding words that do justice to these amazing horses.

This one hurts as much as it did that afternoon in May when I stood in the park crying, knowing my beloved stallion was gone.

How do you say goodbye?

There is truth to Chief Seattle's words:
> "There is no death, only a change of worlds."

We still see Mystery, and all of the others who have passed away, in their favorite areas or the places where we were blessed to share in small moments of their lives. His spirit lives on through his offspring still living in the park: Stallion Half Moon, Mare Sumac, Mare Teepee, Stallion Gunner and Mare Esprit. 2020 added fillies Emery, Birdie and Raven's Myst to that list. I can't tell you how many times Filly Birdie has looked at me and all I see is her daddy looking back at me!

The spirit of this great stallion lives forever in the only home he ever knew where he lived his entire life wild and free.

It is truly an honor to have shared a small part of his life with him.

Rest in Peace Mystery. Thank you for the memories! We really thought we had many more years to share with you!

2020 Filly Birdie

Stallion Mystery

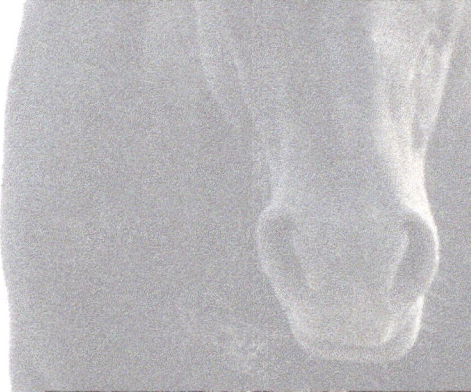

Chasing Horses

NOTES

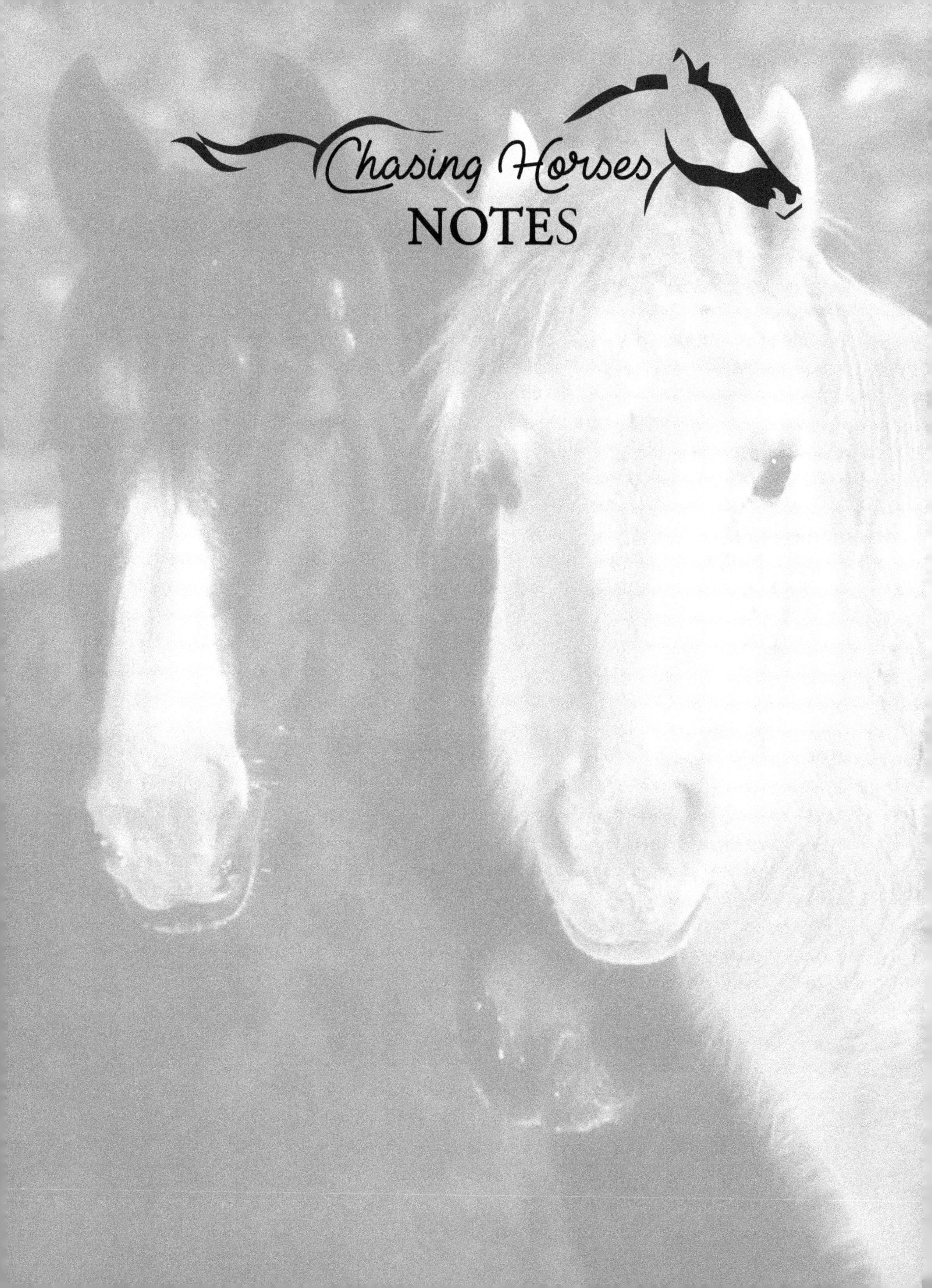

Chasing Horses
NOTES

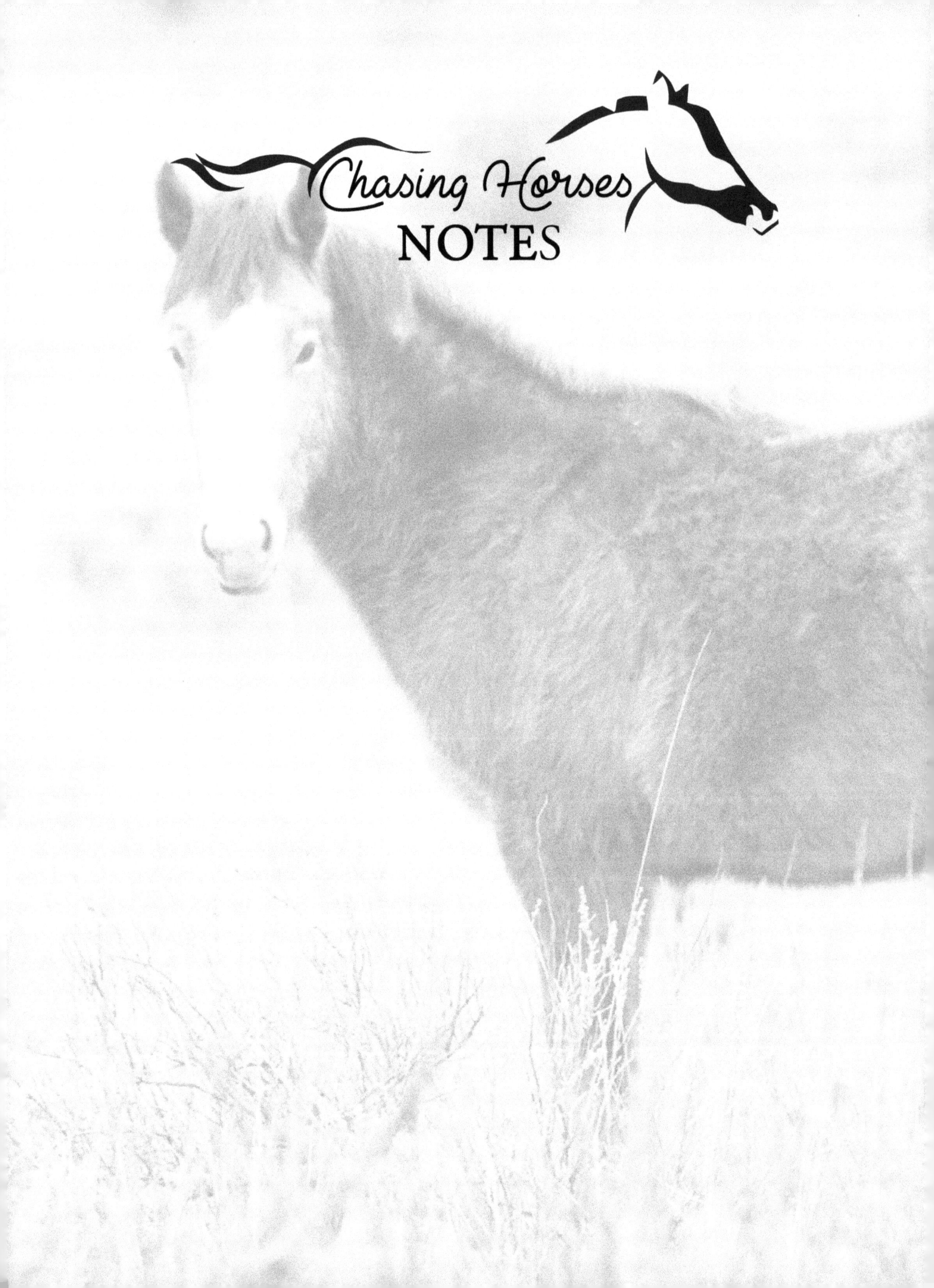

Chasing Horses
NOTES

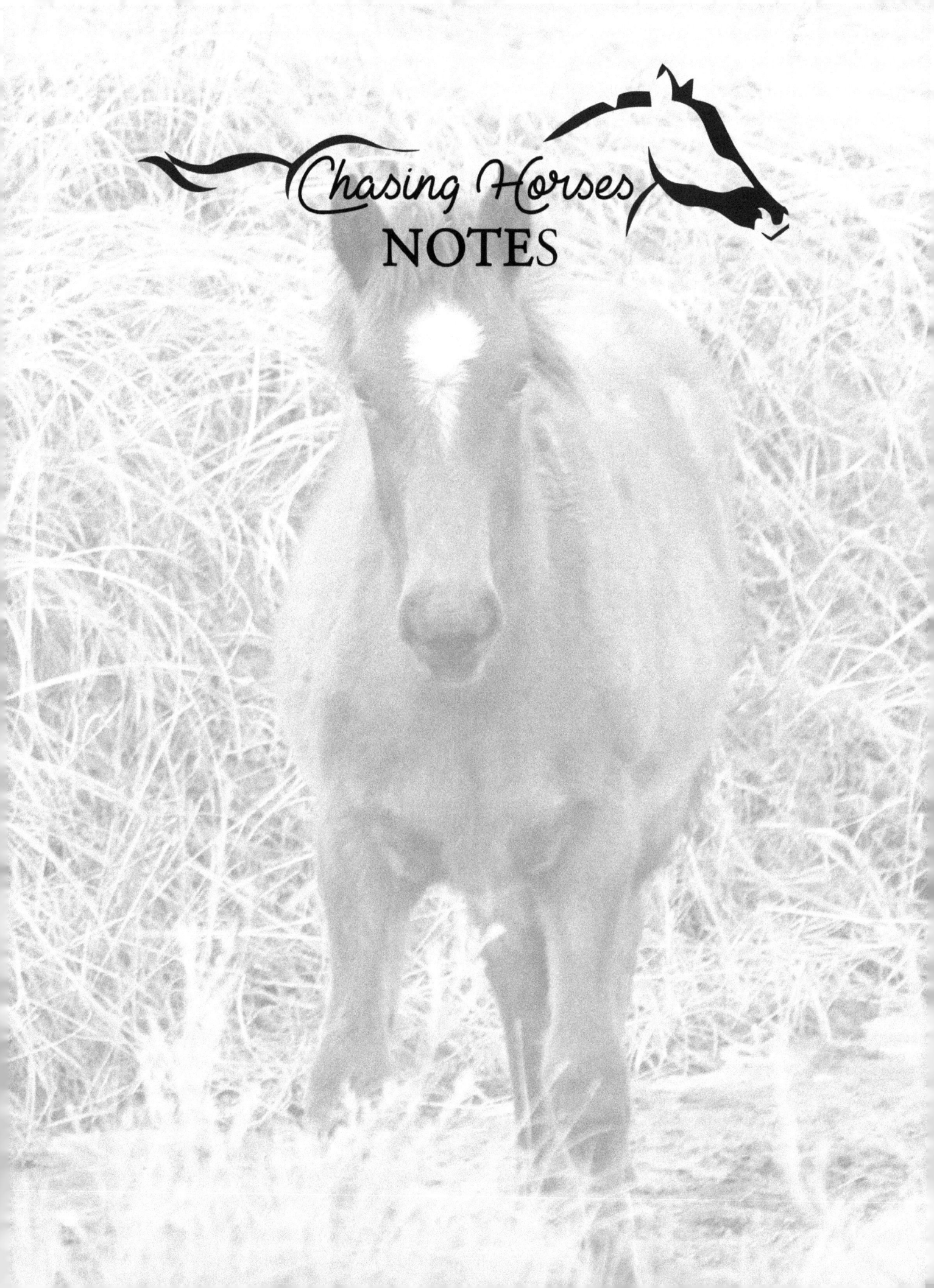

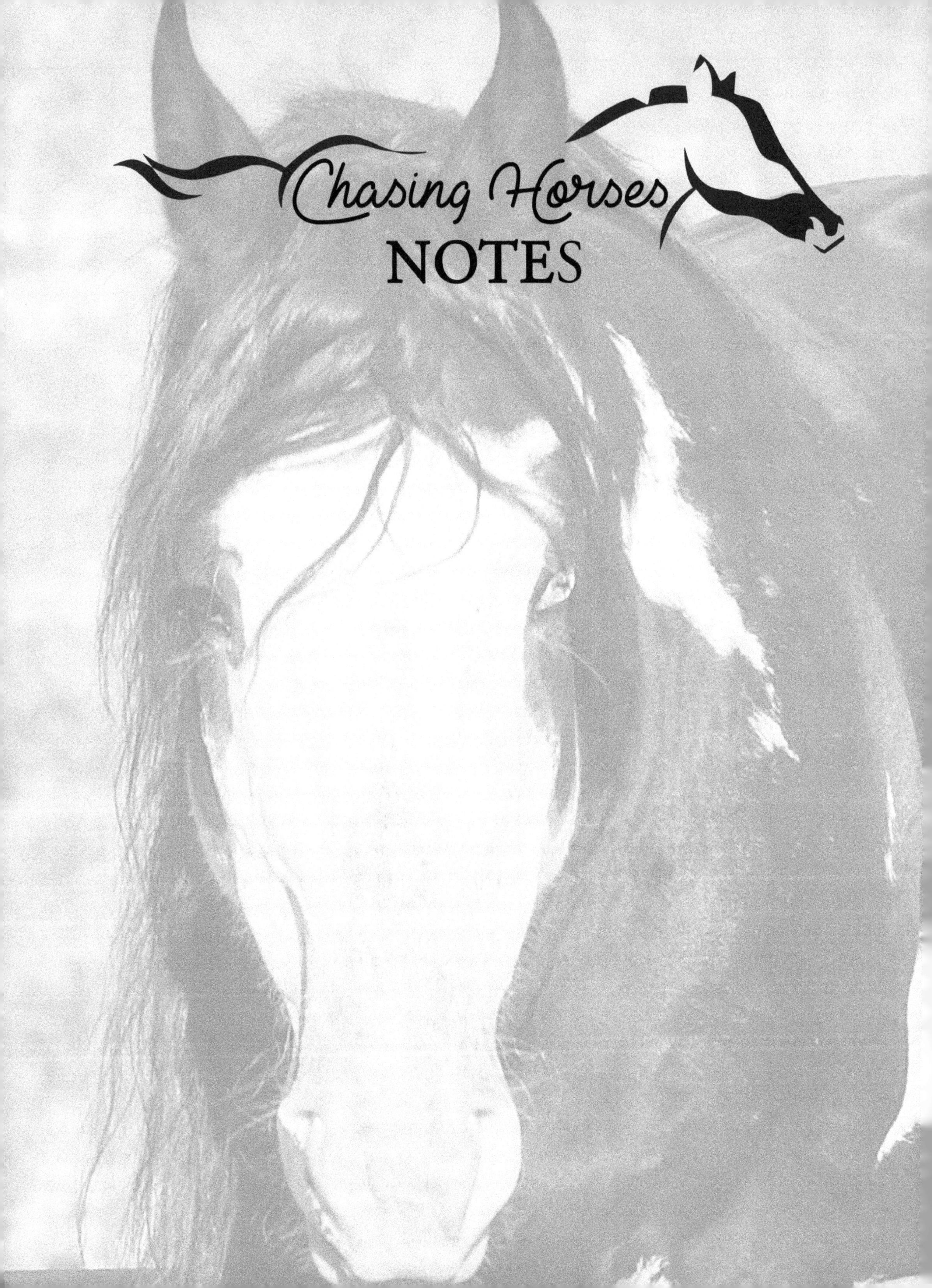

Chasing Horses

NOTES

Want more?
Stay up to date on what happens next
with the horses of
Theodore Roosevelt National Park
by following us on Facebook
(https://www.facebook.com/chasinghorsesnd)
and Instagram @ChasinghorsesND

Thank you for your support!

www.ingramcontent.com/pod-product-compliance
Lightning Source LLC
Chambersburg PA
CBHW040832040426
42336CB00034B/3455